FREE FROM BONDAGE GOD'S WAY

KAY ARTHUR

D0067985

HARVEST HOUSE PUBLISHERS
Eugene, Oregon 97402

Cover illustration and interior art by Micha'el Washer

Cover by Left Coast Design, Portland, Oregon

The International Inductive Study Series
FREE FROM BONDAGE GOD'S WAY

Copyright © 1994 by Precept Ministries
Published by Harvest House Publishers
Eugene, Oregon 97402

Library of Congress Cataloging-in-Publication Data

Arthur, Kay, 1933–
    Free from bondage God's way / Kay Arthur.
       p. cm. — (The International inductive study series)
      ISBN 1-56507-205-7
      1. Bible. N.T. Galatians—Study and teaching. 2. Bible. N.T. Ephesians—
Study and teaching.   I. Title.   II. Series: Arthur, Kay, 1933–
International inductive study series.
BS2685.5.A78   1994
227'.4'007—dc20   94-19165
                                                 CIP

Printed in the United States of America.

99   00   /   BF   /   11   10   9   8   7   6

CONTENTS

How to Get Started...

Sometimes it's hard to read instructions. You simply want to get started, and only if all else fails will you read the directions. I understand, but in this case, don't do it! These instructions are part of getting started, and they will help you greatly.

FIRST

Let's talk about what you are going to need in order to do this study. In addition to this book, you will need four "tools":

1. A Bible (I recommend using an *International Inductive Study Bible* [IISB]. It's ideal for this kind of study because of its easy-to-read type, wide margins, single column text, high-quality paper, and innumerable study helps.)

2. A set of colored pencils or an eight-color Pentel pencil (available at most office supply stores)

3. A composition book or notebook for working on your assignments and recording your insights

4. A four-color ballpoint pen for marking your Bible

SECOND

Though you will be given specific instructions for each day's study, there are basic things you'll want to look for and do as you study each book chapter by chapter. Let me list them for you. Read through the list but don't be overwhelmed. Eventually, each step will become a habit.

1. As you read each chapter, train yourself to ask the "5 W's and an H": who, what, when, where, why, and how. Asking questions like these helps you see exactly what the Word of God is saying. When you interrogate the text with the 5 W's and an H, ask questions like this:

   a. **What** is the chapter about?

   b. **Who** are the main characters?

   c. **When** does this event or teaching take place?

   d. **Where** does this happen?

   e. **Why** is this being done or said?

   f. **How** did it happen?

2. The "when" of events or teachings is very important and should be marked in an easily recognizable way in your Bible. I do this by putting a clock (like the one shown here) in the margin of my Bible beside the verse where the time phrase occurs. You may want to underline or color the references to time in one specific color.

Remember, time may be expressed in several different ways: by mentioning an actual year, month, or day, or by mentioning an event such as a feast, a year of a ruler's reign, etc. Time can also be indicated by words such as *then, when, afterward, at this time,* etc.

3. There are certain key words that you will want to mark in a special way in the text of your Bible. This is the purpose of the colored pencils and the colored pen. Developing the habit of marking your Bible in this way will make

a significant difference in the way you study and in how much you remember.

A **key word** is an important word that is used by the author repeatedly in order to convey his message to his reader. Certain key words will show up throughout the book as a whole, while other key words will be concentrated in certain chapters or segments of the book. You will want to mark key words and their relative pronouns (*he, his, she, her, it, we, they, us, our, you, them, their*) as well as any synonyms in a distinguishable color or way.

For instance, one of the key words in Galatians is *gospel*. I put a hot-pink megaphone like this ⟨gospel⟩ around the word *gospel* and then color it in with green. I use the megaphone because God tells us we are to proclaim the gospel.

You need to devise a color-coding system for key words so that when you look at a page of your Bible, you will instantly see where a particular word is used. When you start marking key words in various colors and symbols, it is easy to forget how you are marking certain words. Therefore, you will find it helpful to take a three-by-five or five-by-seven card, cut it in half lengthwise, write the key words on the card, color code them, and then use the card as a bookmark as you work your way through the book you are studying.

Like *gospel*, *covenant* is also a key word in the study of Galatians. I mark the word *covenant* the same way throughout my Bible: I color it red and box it in yellow. I mark the word *grace* blue and box it in yellow. *Grace* will be a very important word in Galatians and Ephesians. And references to the devil and his cohorts can easily be seen in my Bible because I mark these with a red pitchfork ⟋⟍. You will mark some references to the devil in Ephesians. Marking words for easy identification can be done by colors, symbols, or a combination of colors and symbols. However, colors are easier to distinguish than symbols. If I use symbols, I keep them very simple. For example, I color *repent* yellow but put a red arrow over it also: repent . The symbol conveys the meaning of repent: a change of mind.

When I mark the members of the Godhead (which I do not always mark), I color every reference to the Father, Son, and Holy Spirit in yellow. I also use a purple pen and mark the Father with a triangle △, symbolizing the Trinity. I mark the Son this way⎯, and the Holy Spirit this way.

When you are instructed to mark a key word, the word is the *New American Standard* translation of the word. However, if the *King James Version* (KJV), the *New King James Version* (NKJV), or *New International Version* (NIV) translates the word differently, the word used in those translations is given to you in a footnote.

4. Because locations are important in a historical or biographical book of the Bible and in the first two chapters of Galatians, you will also find it helpful to mark these in a distinguishable way. I simply underline every reference to location in green (grass and trees are green!), using my four-color ballpoint pen.

I also look up the locations on maps so I can put myself into context geographically. You'll do this in the first two chapters of Galatians. (If you have an *International Inductive Study Bible* you will find the pertinent maps placed right in the text where you need them as a ready reference.)

5. When you finish studying a chapter, record the main theme of that chapter on the AT A GLANCE chart provided for you under the appropriate chapter number. (If you

have an IISB, you will want to record the chapter themes on the AT A GLANCE chart at the end of each book in your Bible. Then you will have a permanent record of your studies right at your fingertips.)

6. If you are doing this study within the framework of a class and you find the lessons too heavy, then simply do what you can. To do a little is better than to do nothing. Don't be an "all or nothing" person when it comes to Bible study.

Remember, any time you get into the Word of God, you enter into more intensive warfare with the enemy. Why? Every piece of the Christian's armor is related to the Word of God. And our one and only offensive weapon is the sword of the Spirit, which is the Word of God. The enemy wants you to have a dull sword. Don't cooperate! You don't have to! How well you will see this in your study of Ephesians.

7. Always begin your studies with prayer. As you do your part to handle the Word of God accurately, you must remember that the Bible is a divinely inspired book. The words that you are reading are truth, given to you by God that you might know Him and His ways. These truths are divinely revealed: "For to us God revealed them through the Spirit; for the Spirit searches all things, even the depths of God. For who among men knows the thoughts of a man except the spirit of the man, which is in him? Even so the thoughts of God no one knows except the Spirit of God" (1 Corinthians 2:10,11).

Therefore, ask God to reveal His truth to you, to lead you and guide you into all truth. He will, if you will ask.

THIRD

This study is designed to put you into the Word of God on a *daily* basis. Since man does not live by bread alone but by every word that comes out of the mouth of God, we each need a daily helping.

The assignments for each week cover seven days; however, the seventh day is different from the other days. On the seventh day, the focus is on a major truth covered in that week's study.

You will find a verse or two to memorize and STORE IN YOUR HEART. Then there is a passage to READ AND DISCUSS. This will be extremely profitable for those who are using this material in a class setting, for it will cause the class to focus their attention on a critical portion of Scripture. To aid the individual and/or the class, there's a set of OPTIONAL QUESTIONS FOR DISCUSSION. This is followed with a THOUGHT FOR THE WEEK which will help you understand how to walk in the light of what you learned.

When you discuss the week's lesson, be sure to support your answers and insights from the Bible itself. Then you will be handling the Word of God in a way that will find His approval. Always examine your insights by carefully observing the text to see *what it says*. Then, before you decide *what a Scripture or passage means*, make sure you interpret it in the light of its context.

Scripture will never contradict Scripture. If it ever seems to, you can be certain that somewhere something is being taken out of context. If you come to a passage that is difficult to deal with, reserve your interpretations for a time when you can study the passage in greater depth.

Books in *The International Inductive Study Series* are survey courses. If you want to do a more in-depth study of a particular book of the Bible, we would suggest you do a Precept Upon Precept Bible Study Course on that book. You may obtain more information on these studies by contacting Precept Ministries, P.O. Box 182218, Chattanooga, TN 37422, 423/892-6814, or by filling out and mailing the response card in this book.

Free from Bondage God's Way...

- We're listening to the messages of others, but we're not learning the Bible.
- We can quote truth, but we really can't explain it... and we're having trouble living it out.
- We're ready to state our theological position, but we can't defend it by reasoning from the whole counsel of the Word of God.

Many are being led astray by every wind of doctrine and cunning craftiness of men (Ephesians 4:14).

We live in a time when many who proclaim Christ don't hunger and thirst for sound doctrine. Instead they love to have their ears tickled. They want to hear some new revelation, some new insight—something different. Something that appeals to their senses and their desires.

"Capture my attention with a good story."

"Don't go too deep. I've had to think all day."

"Show me how this will meet my needs... solve my problems... give me a quick fix without too much commitment on my part."

"What I want is a solution. And I need it now!"

What is the problem?

Mankind is in bondage. Some people are in bondage to Satan, and thus to self and sin. Others are in bondage, held

11

captive by the enemy's lies, because they don't know truth. Still others are in bondage to the law or to a legalistic style of Christianity that snuffs the life and joy out of their walk with the Lord Jesus Christ.

What—*who*—can set us free?

That, Beloved, is what this study of Galatians and Ephesians is all about. "It was for freedom that Christ set us free" (Galatians 5:1). Therefore, no child of God is to live in bondage. Jesus came to set the captive free. Freedom comes from knowing truth. Truth is a person—Jesus is the way, the truth and the life (John 14:6). And His word is truth. Thus, Jesus prayed, "Sanctify them in the truth; Thy word is truth" (John 17:17).

This, my friend, is also my prayer for you as you begin this study of Galatians and Ephesians. I pray that you will know, through the Word of truth, the freedom that is yours in Christ Jesus—and that by faith you will walk in that freedom.

GALATIANS

Saved by Grace
but in Bondage to the Law?

DAY ONE

In this first week you will discover the purpose of this epistle (letter) to the Galatians. Asking pertinent questions will help you pinpoint its purpose. Who wrote Galatians? Why was it written? To whom was it written? And what is so important about the book of Galatians? Why did God want this epistle to be a permanent part of the Word of God?

When you answer these last questions, you will see why you need to understand the message of Galatians and live accordingly.

This study is going to be wonderfully freeing!

When you study a book of the Bible, it is always best to first read it straight through without stopping. In doing this, you gain a sense of the entire message of the book, which provides you with a good overview. If you have time today, read through Galatians but do not mark anything. Then return to the first chapter and simply complete today's assignment.

Read Galatians 1:1-10 and color every reference to the recipients of this letter in one color. Watch for and mark the pronouns *you* or *us* as they refer to the recipients of Galatians. Marking references to the recipients allows you to go back later and note from each what you learn about them. This exercise will help you see the author's purpose for writing this very needful epistle. You will see then that Christians today deal with the same problems the Galatians had.

In your notebook, begin a list of what you learn from marking these references to the recipients. As you finish each day's assignment, look back at any references to the recipients you have marked. Read them carefully; add what you learn about those who received this letter to the list in your notebook. At the end of the week, you will be amazed at all you have learned about these people!

As you read 1:1-10, also mark the word *grace* in one distinctive way and the word *gospel* in another. These two key words will help unlock the purpose and meaning of the book of Galatians.

Today and this week, also watch for answers to the following questions:

a. **Who** wrote Galatians? *Paul*

b. **To whom** was Galatians written? *R+ m G.*

c. **Why** was Galatians written? **What** is its purpose? *false gospel being preached, emphasize True gospel, the only Gospel*

Record the answers in your notebook. Then transfer them to the GALATIANS AT A GLANCE chart (page 42). You will continue to add information to this chart as we work our way through the book. This information will then always be at your fingertips!

DAY TWO

Read Galatians 1:11–2:21. Continue to mark the words *grace* and *gospel*, but also add to these the word *Law*.[1] I mark the word *Law* like this Law , because it reminds me of the Ten Commandments written on stone tablets.

At this point you may want to make your three-by-five card mentioned in the section "How to Get Started."

Also don't forget to mark the references to the recipients and to add to your list what you learn about them from simply observing the text.

DAY THREE

Today read Galatians 3. At this point add another key word, *Spirit*, and continue marking all the key words. Remember, I color references to the Holy Spirit yellow and put a diagram like this ◢◣◣◢ around it.

---

[1] NIV; KJV; NKJV: *law*

Don't forget to add *Spirit* to your bookmark. Add any insights on the recipients to your list. Remember, your goal is to discover what you can about Galatians and to understand why this epistle was written.

DAY FOUR

On this fourth day, read Galatians 4. If the following key words are used, mark them: *grace, gospel, Law,* and *Spirit.*

As you read and mark, think about what you are reading and marking. The Bible is God's handbook for life. God wants to speak to your heart, and He will—if you will listen.

DAY FIVE

Read Galatians 5 today and mark any key words. Don't forget to mark the references to the recipients and to add what you learn about them to your list.

DAY SIX

Read Galatians 6 today and once again mark the references to the recipients and the key words on your list. When you finish, go through the book of Galatians and notice every time you have marked the word *gospel.* In your notebook, make a list of what you learn from Galatians about the gospel.

DAY SEVEN

Store in your heart: Galatians 1:8.

Read and discuss: Galatians 1:1-10 and what you marked

with respect to the Galatians. Go over the lists you made about the recipients and about the gospel.

OPTIONAL QUESTIONS FOR DISCUSSION

[handwritten: Paul] ∾ Who wrote the epistle to the Galatians?

[handwritten: false gospel] ∾ What do you learn about the Galatians? What were they dealing with? What had happened to them? As you give your answer, support it from the text of Galatians. Tell where you got your insight.

∾ Do you know any people who are having to deal with the same issues that the Galatians faced? *[handwritten: those involved in cults]*

[handwritten: Gentiles had to be circumcised (under Law)] ∾ The title of this study book on Galatians and Ephesians is *Free from Bondage God's Way.* Do you sense that the Galatians were under any sort of bondage? If so, what was it? Can you relate in any way? *[handwritten: judaizers.]*

∾ What did you learn about the gospel from marking every reference to it in the book of Galatians?

∾ From the book of Galatians, what do you see as your own responsibility with respect to the gospel?

[handwritten: keep it pure - keep it simple. He crucified (for sin: no other one needed!)]

THOUGHT FOR THE WEEK

When we seek to put people under a legalistic set of rules such as "do not handle, do not taste, do not touch" (Colossians 2:21), are we distorting the gospel of Jesus Christ? Do such rules put people under a form of bondage that keeps them from understanding and walking in the grace of God?

Is it by the law that someone gains favor in the sight of God? Is it by the law that someone maintains his Christian testimony? Is it by the power of the law that a child of God controls the desires of his flesh?

[handwritten: Walk in the Spirit not legalism]

These, Beloved, are questions you need to think about. You need God's answers to these questions because I'm sure you don't want to distort God's gospel in any way.

Shackled by Your Past?

DAY ONE

This week we want to take a good look at Paul, the one who wrote the epistle to the Galatians. Not only is there much to learn about Paul, there is also much to learn from his example. Paul challenged the Corinthians to be imitators of him, even as he was of Christ Jesus (1 Corinthians 11:1).

Read Galatians 1. Watch the progression of events in Paul's life. Mark every reference to time in a distinctive way or color. You may want to put a clock like this ⏰ in the margin of your Bible next to the verse that contains the reference to time.

List in your notebook what you learn about Paul from this chapter. Save space for other insights you'll want to add to this list later.

DAY TWO

Read Galatians 2. Once again observe the references to time and the sequence of events. Add what you learn about Paul to your list.

To gain a good overview of Paul's life and ministry, study the chart called SEQUENCE OF EVENTS IN PAUL'S LIFE AFTER HIS CONVERSION (page 26). Then look at the map on page 22 to note many of the places Paul journeyed. If a place noted on the chart SEQUENCE OF EVENTS IN PAUL'S LIFE AFTER HIS CONVERSION is mentioned in Galatians, highlight or color that location on the map. (You will not find the region of Judea.)

Paul's Travels as a New Believer

DAY THREE

Read Galatians 1:11-17 again. This time as you read, think about when God really knew Paul. When did He set Paul apart? What was He going to do with Paul? Compare this passage with Ephesians 1:1-5. Think about what you learn about salvation from these two passages.

Then read Psalm 139:1-17. What do you learn about God and about yourself in these verses? Does this passage relate in any way to what you just read in Galatians and Ephesians? Think about it, Beloved.

DAY FOUR

Read through Galatians 1:11-17 again. Then read Acts 9:1-25 and note how the verses in Acts complement and expand your understanding of Paul's conversion.

As you do this week's study, you may want to write the cross-references you study today and the next two days in the margin of your Bible. In days to come, you'll be glad you did this. You don't always have all your notes with you, but if you write the cross-references in your Bible you don't have to be concerned. They are there for a ready reference.

To mark cross-references, you would write Acts 9:1-25 in the margin somewhere next to Galatians 1:11-17. Then at Acts 9:1-25 you would write Galatians 1:11-17. This is how you do cross-references.

DAY FIVE

As you continue to take a closer look at Paul, read Galatians 1:18-24 and Acts 9:26-30. As you read and think about Paul's beginning as a new creation in Christ Jesus, keep in mind the chart SEQUENCE OF EVENTS IN PAUL'S LIFE AFTER HIS CONVERSION (page 26).

DAY SIX

Read through Galatians 2 again marking every occurrence of the word *justified* and note how a man is justified. The word *justified* means "to be declared righteous." Compare Galatians 2 with Acts 15:1-33.

How would you summarize the content of Galatians 1 and 2? What is the main theme or subject of each of these first two chapters? Record the theme of each chapter under the respective chapter number on the GALATIANS AT A GLANCE chart on page 42.

DAY SEVEN

Store in your heart: Galatians 1:15,16.

Read and discuss: Galatians 1:11-24; Philippians 3:4-7; Acts 9:1-22.

Summary of Paul's background
Paul's background
Paul's conversion
receiving 'sight'
Paul's obedience to Lord
Damascus / Jerusalem :30 (Tarsus)

OPTIONAL QUESTIONS FOR DISCUSSION

ꙮ What about Paul's conversion interested you most? Why?

ꙮ What was Paul like before he became a Christian? Remember to look at Philippians 3:4-7.

ꙮ According to Galatians 1:15,16, why was Paul not saved earlier—for instance, when Jesus was still living? What can you learn about salvation from this account?

ꙮ Would the same timing of salvation (when it pleased God) apply to you? Although you may not understand the full theological ramifications of this truth, does this knowledge comfort you in any way? How?

ꙮ As Paul gives his personal testimony and account of some incidents that occurred after his conversion, why do you think he shared the controversy he had with Peter with the Galatians? What was his purpose?

ꙮ Look at the chart SEQUENCE OF EVENTS IN PAUL'S LIFE AFTER HIS CONVERSION (page 26), and note what you see about Paul's faithfulness to God's calling on his life. What do you see that you can "imitate"?

THOUGHT FOR THE WEEK

Have you wept over your past and been, in a sense, tormented in your thoughts because you didn't come to know Jesus earlier? Rest, beloved child of God, for God saved you when it pleased Him. His promise is there to comfort and assure you that the Sovereign God—the God of all flesh—is able to cause all things, even your "before Christ" days, to work together for good. He will use them to make you like Jesus.

So, like Paul, take God at His Word. He does not lie. He stands by His Word to perform it. Forget those things which are past and press on toward the prize of the high calling of God in Christ Jesus (Philippians 3:7-14). You are His workmanship, created in Christ Jesus for good works which God has fore-ordained for you to walk in (Ephesians 2:10). Go forward in faith.

Sequence of Events in Paul's Life after His Conversion*

*There are differing opinions on these dates. For continuity's sake this chart will be the basis for dates pertaining to Paul's life.

Year A.D.	Event
33-34	Conversion, time in Damascus
35-47	Some silent years, except we know that Paul:
	1. Spent time in Arabia and Damascus
	2. Made first visit to Jerusalem
	3. Went to Tarsus, Syria-Cilicia area
	4. Was with Barnabas in Antioch
	5. With Barnabas took relief to brethren in Judea—Paul's second visit to Jerusalem
	6. Returned to Antioch; was sent out with Barnabas by church at Antioch
47-48	**First missionary journey:** Galatians written(?)
49	Apostolic Council at Jerusalem—Paul visits Jerusalem (compare Acts 15 with Galatians 2:1)
49-51	**Second missionary journey:** 1 and 2 Thessalonians written
52-56	**Third missionary journey:** 1 and 2 Corinthians and Romans written
56	Paul goes to Jerusalem and is arrested; held at Caesarea
57-59	Appearance before Felix and Drusilla; before Festus; before Agrippa
59-60	Appeals to Caesar, sent from Caesarea to Rome
60-62	First Roman imprisonment: Ephesians, Philemon, Colossians, and Philippians written
62	Paul's release; possible trip to Spain
62	Paul in Macedonia: 1 Timothy written
62	Paul goes to Crete: Titus written
63-64	Paul taken to Rome and imprisoned: 2 Timothy written
64	Paul is absent from the body and present with the Lord
	(Others put Paul's conversion about A.D. 35, his death in A.D. 68.)

Where's Freedom from Your Flesh?

DAY ONE

Read Galatians 2:11–3:5 so you see the flow of thought from Galatians 2 to Galatians 3. Think about it. Add the word *faith*[2] to your list of key words on your bookmark. Now read 2:11–3:5 again and mark the key words.

DAY TWO

Add the word *promise(s)* to your list of key words on your bookmark. Read Galatians 3 and mark the key words. You will see in Galatians 3:8 that the word *justify* is used. Since you have been marking *justified*, you should also mark *justify* in this verse. This form of the word is only used this one time in the book. Watch the flow of thought.

DAY THREE

Read Galatians 3:1-5 and Ephesians 1:13,14. Record in your notebook what you learn from these passages about the Galatians and about the Spirit.

---

[2]NIV: *Faith* is also translated *believing* and *believes*, so you should mark these also.

DAY FOUR

Read Galatians 3:5-14 and Genesis 12:1-3. List in your notebook what you learn about Abraham. Note who his sons were.

DAY FIVE

Add the word *covenant* to your bookmark. Read Galatians 3:13-18 and mark key words. Then read Genesis 15:1-6,18 and Romans 4:1-9. Record in your notebook what you learn from these passages about how Abraham was made righteous.

DAY SIX

Read Galatians 3:19-29 and mark any key words you may have missed on Day Two. In your notebook list what you learn about the law and why it was given.

How would you summarize the content of Galatians 3? Record the theme of this chapter on the appropriate line of the GALATIANS AT A GLANCE chart (page 42).

DAY SEVEN

Store in your heart: Galatians 3:23,24.
Read and discuss: Galatians 3:10-26 and James 2:10.

OPTIONAL QUESTIONS FOR DISCUSSION

∾ What did you learn from marking the words *justified* and *justify* in Galatians 2 and 3? According to God's Word, how is a person justified (made righteous) before God?

∾ What did you learn about the law from Galatians 2 and Paul's relationship to the law? What was his relationship to it like before he met Christ and what was it like after?

∽ According to James 2:10, if you live under the law, what is your obligation to the law?

∽ In light of what you saw in Galatians 3, answer the following questions:

   a. Which came first, God's promise to Abraham or the law?

   b. Did the coming of the law (400 years after God's promise to Abraham) cancel out God's promise to Abraham? *No*

   c. What is the purpose of the law? *brought to*

   d. When you come to Christ, what is your relationship to the law? *no longer under law*

   e. What problem were the Galatians having in relation to the law?

∽ Where are you in your relationship with God? Have you been justified by faith so that you are now crucified with Christ and living by faith? If you have been justified by faith, are you living by faith? Or have you slipped back under the law, so that your relationship with God is based on performance rather than faith? Do you think you're perfected by the performance of your flesh?

THOUGHT FOR THE WEEK

Keeping your set of "laws" can't change you and give you an inner sense of being right with God, can it, my friend? No matter how hard you try, no matter how much you go through your form of worship (whatever it is), no matter how much you try to obey the laws of your religion or try only to do good deeds instead of bad ones, there is no peace inside nor victory over your own flesh, is there? There is no freedom from your flesh and its desires, is there?

Only faith in Jesus Christ has set you free or can set you free. And since that is true, why then do you think you can do what you couldn't do before? Why do you think you can make yourself perfect, pleasing, acceptable to God by the strength of your flesh!

If you have truly believed in the Lord Jesus Christ, then you are under a new covenant—a covenant that gives you the Spirit of God to live within you.

Don't allow yourself to come under bondage again!

WEEK FOUR

You're an Heir of Grace . . . Live Like It!

DAY ONE

Add *heir*[3] to your bookmark. Read Galatians 4 and mark key words.

DAY TWO

Read Galatians 4:1-11 again. In your notebook list everything you learn about our adoption as sons.

DAY THREE

Read Galatians 4:12-31. Note what you learn about Paul and his concern in this passage because of Galatians 4:15 and Galatians 6:11. Some believe that Paul's bodily illness may have been related to his eyes. Perhaps Paul's reference to his "thorn in the flesh" in 2 Corinthians 12:7-10 is related to his illness also.

DAY FOUR

Read Hebrews 8. Mark the word *covenant.* Be aware that

---

[3]NIV: The word *heir* is translated *inheritance* in 4:30.

there are references to both the first covenant (the law) and the second or new covenant (of grace). Distinguish between these by the way you mark each. In your notebook, list what you learn about these covenants from this chapter.

DAY FIVE

Add the word *flesh*[4] to your bookmark. Read Galatians 4:21-31 and mark *flesh*. Also make sure you mark the word *covenants*. [5]

By the way, watch the words *free* and *freedom* in this passage. Then go back and look at Galatians 2:4 and 4:3-7. Compare our freedom with what held us in bondage. Notice who and what covenant set us free. This is freedom from bondage God's way!

DAY SIX

Read Genesis 16:1-6,15,16; 17:15-21; 21:1-13. Then read Galatians 4:21-31 again. Now on a page in your notebook make a chart with two headings: HAGAR'S SON and SARAH'S SON. Then under these headings list what you learn from Galatians 4:21-31 about both of these sons.

Now how would you summarize the content of Galatians 4? Record the theme of this chapter on the appropriate line of the GALATIANS AT A GLANCE chart (page 42).

DAY SEVEN

Store in your heart: Galatians 4:31.
Read and discuss: Galatians 4:21-31 and 5:1.

---

[4]NIV: Mark *in the ordinary way* in Galatians 4 and *sinful nature* in Galatians 5 and 6.
[5]NIV: Also mark *covenant*.

OPTIONAL QUESTIONS FOR DISCUSSION

∾ What did you learn about Abraham's two sons from Genesis?

∾ What did you learn about Hagar's son and Sarah's son?

∾ What parallels do you see from what you learned in Galatians and Genesis with respect to Abraham's sons and
Abraham's relationship to them and to their mothers?

∾ Discuss again what you learned about the recipients of this
epistle and why Paul wrote to them. Discuss the allegory
Paul uses; talk about why you feel he uses it and about how
it helps him achieve his purpose.

∾ According to what we have studied in Galatians, what is
the bondage from which Jesus Christ sets us free?

∾ If you belong to Jesus Christ, are you a slave or an heir?
How are you living in your relationship to your God?

THOUGHT FOR THE WEEK

There is nothing more debilitating in your relationship
with God than to think you please God only when you keep
your own little spiritual list of do's and don'ts or someone else's
list which has been imposed on you. When you feel God will
only bless you when you don't cross any of your man-made
religious boundaries, you live in bondage to legalism or to the
law.

If you belong to God through faith in Jesus Christ, then,
my friend, you are a beloved child of God. You are His heir
forever. You are the child of the free woman. Jerusalem is your
home. You are not under condemnation. God's blessing for you
is that of grace, not performance. You are an heir according to
God's unchangeable promise. The Holy Spirit dwells within
you and will never leave you nor forsake you. You will live with
God forever and ever. You will never be cast out. So cast out

the bondwoman and her son. You are under grace not law, and when you walk in that grace you will be all you should and can be. Grace doesn't make you lawless; it simply sets you free from bondage God's way, so you can live a life that is pleasing to God.

WEEK FIVE

How Do You Walk by the Spirit?

DAY ONE

Read Galatians 5 and mark any key words. Also make sure you mark every reference to the recipients of this epistle.

DAY TWO

Read Galatians 5:1-12 and mark the words *circumcision*[6] and *love*.

DAY THREE

Read Genesis 17:9-14. Mark the words *covenant* and *circumcised* and notice the relationship of covenant and circumcision. Write what you learn in your notebook.

DAY FOUR

Read Galatians 1:6-10; 3:1; 4:17; 5:7-12; and 6:12,13,17. Mark every occurrence of the word *circumcision* or *circumcised*. (You will not find the word used in each reference, only in a

---

[6]NIV; KJV; NKJV: Also mark *circumcised*.

couple.) List in your notebook what you learn about those who opposed Paul's teaching.

DAY FIVE

Read Galatians 5:13-15 and Mark 12:28-34, marking every occurrence of the word *love*.

DAY SIX

Read Galatians 5:16-26. Make sure you have marked every occurrence of the word *flesh*.[7] List in your notebook what you learn about the flesh and the Spirit.

Record the theme of Galatians 5 on the appropriate line of the GALATIANS AT A GLANCE chart (page 42).

DAY SEVEN

Store in your heart: Galatians 5:16.
Read and discuss: Galatians 5:16-26.

OPTIONAL QUESTIONS FOR DISCUSSION

∞ What did you learn this week about Paul's opposition? Who is his opposition? What are they called? What position or teaching do you think they hold?

∞ So often the phrase "fallen from grace" is taken out of its context and used to teach that people can lose their salvation. When you see this phrase in its context in Galatians 5, what do you think it means?

---

[7]NIV: *sinful nature*

∾ If those of "the circumcision" were teaching salvation by grace (faith) but still held that circumcision and adherence to the law were required for salvation, what would people who believed their teaching be under? *Law*

∾ If you are under the law, can you also be under grace? Are the two compatible? *No*

∾ Does freedom from the law allow a Christian to live a life controlled by the flesh? *No*

    a. What are the deeds or works of the flesh?

    b. What keeps a child of God from walking by the flesh?

    c. Can a child of God live haphazardly, i.e., any way he wants once he is saved, or does he need to make a very definite choice in the way he walks? According to Galatians 5, how is he to walk?

    d. What has a child of God done with respect to the flesh? *crucified*

∾ The verb *practice*[8] in Galatians 5:21 is in the present tense, which indicates continuous action. Does the usage of this verb then imply that a child of God can never do any of these things, or does it imply that it won't be his habit of life? If it is his habit of life, what does this tell you about his relationship to Jesus Christ? Is it genuine?

∾ Read Galatians 5:22,23. Are there nine fruits of the Spirit or is there one fruit of the Spirit with nine manifestations? The text tells you. Look carefully at the subject and the verb. Are they singular or plural?

    a. Discuss the fruit of the Spirit.

    b. If a person is under the control of the Spirit, would he be living an unrighteous lifestyle? *No*

---

[8]NIV: *live like this*; KJV: *do*

THOUGHT FOR THE WEEK

Beloved, if you see the inability of the law to make you righteous, how can you think you need the law to sustain your righteousness once you come to Jesus? Can the law perfect you before God? When you enter into the new covenant of grace, you receive the promise of the Holy Spirit! Don't quench or grieve the precious Spirit of God! Let Him control your life, conquer sin, and bring forth His fruit—that of Christlikeness.

You are saved and given life by the Spirit—now habitually walk under His control.

If you say, "But I can't!" then it is quite possible that you have never been truly saved, born again of the Spirit. Ask God to show you the condition of your heart.

Bearing the Cross...
and His Brandmarks

DAY ONE

Add the word *cross* to your bookmark. Read Galatians 6 and mark the key words. List in your notebook what you learn from marking *cross* in this chapter. Then go back and read Galatians 2:20 again. According to what you have seen from marking the word *cross* and reading about the Christian's "crucifixion," what place does the cross have in the life of the believer?

DAY TWO

Read Galatians 6:1-5 and Matthew 18:15-20. What do you learn from these passages about how to handle a brother (or sister) who is in sin? Record your insights in your notebook or summarize what you see in the margin of your Bible.

DAY THREE

Read Galatians 6:6-10 and 1 Thessalonians 5:12,13. List in your notebook the ways you can do good to others. Put this truth into practice, even today.

DAY FOUR

Read Galatians 6:11-16. Mark the phrase *new creation*.[9] According to this passage, what matters—being circumcised or being a new creation?

DAY FIVE

Read Romans 7:1-6 and 2 Corinthians 5:17. Mark the words *law* and *new* or *newness* when they appear. (Hint: You will not find all three words in each passage.) Then in your notebook write down how Romans 7 illustrates the Christian's relationship to the law. Who dies—the law or the child of God? Who is made new?

DAY SIX

Read Galatians 6:11-18 and Jeremiah 9:23,24. Mark the word *boast*[10] and note what a Christian is to boast about. Can you boast about this, or do you boast in other things?

Record the theme of Galatians 6 on the appropriate line of the GALATIANS AT A GLANCE chart (page 42). Then fill in as much of the information as you can on this chart. When you finish, you will have a nice summary of the book.

DAY SEVEN

Store in your heart: Galatians 6:14.
Read and discuss: Galatians 6:1-10.

---

[9]KJV: *new creature*
[10]KJV: *glory*

OPTIONAL QUESTIONS FOR DISCUSSION

∞ What did you learn from the book of Galatians about the place of the cross in the life of a believer? To what are we crucified?

∞ How would remembering that you are crucified with Christ help you in your daily walk as a child of God?

∞ According to Galatians 6:16 what will this consciousness of the cross bring to your life?

∞ What is to be our relationship to others according to Galatians 6? How do you live this truth out practically? Discuss it.

∞ If you have time, it would be wonderful to review Galatians chapter by chapter. Think through the content of each chapter from memory. Then you might discuss the following:

a. What do you learn from Galatians, chapter by chapter, about our Lord Jesus Christ?

b. What does our Lord set us free from and how can this knowledge be applied practically?

∞ Finally, have the members of the group share the most significant truth they learned in this study and how it affected their lives or understanding.

THOUGHT FOR THE WEEK

Now, Beloved, walk in the righteous freedom that is yours in Christ Jesus. Don't let anyone put you under the yoke of bondage. Instead take His yoke upon you and learn of Him. Truth sets you free!

GALATIANS AT A GLANCE

Theme of Galatians:

SEGMENT DIVISIONS

		CHAPTER THEMES
		1
		2
		3
		4
		5
		6

Author: Paul / all brethren

Date:

Purpose: keep to true gospel

Key Words: Grace Gospel

EPHESIANS

Why Are You in Bondage to Others' Opinions of You?

DAY ONE

Whenever you study any book of the Bible, it's good to familiarize yourself with the general content of the book before beginning to look at it chapter by chapter, verse by verse. Therefore, today read straight through the book of Ephesians. As you read, watch for the chapter where the author turns from talking about our position *in Christ* to our walk *with* Him. When you finish reading the book, record your answers to the following in your notebook.

a. Who wrote Ephesians? *Paul*

b. To whom was it written? *saints at Ephesus*

c. In what chapter does the book turn from talking about our position in Christ to our walk with Christ? *4*

DAY TWO

Paul visited Ephesus for the first time on his second missionary journey. A brief account of his trip is recorded in Acts 18:18-21. Then on his third missionary journey, Paul returned to Ephesus.

Acts 19 gives some interesting insights into his return visit to Ephesus. It also reveals the background of the Ephesians and Paul's intent in writing the epistle to them. Today, carefully read Acts 19 with these thoughts in mind.

As you read, list in your notebook what you learn from this chapter about the Ephesians. Note what their city is like, what the people are like, how they live, and what they worship. Also note how they respond to the gospel and to Paul.

Look at the map below and locate Ephesus. You see it in what we now know as the country of Turkey.

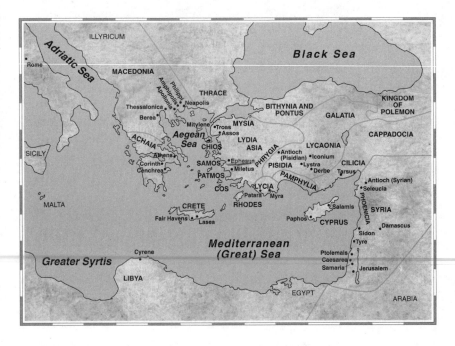

DAY THREE

The people in Ephesus had been in great bondage to the enemy. Therefore Paul wants them to understand two things:

what God did for them, and the blessings that are theirs
through faith in the Lord Jesus Christ. Read Ephesians 1:1-14
and mark any reference to God with a triangle. Also be sure to
watch for and mark personal pronouns (He, His, Him, etc.)
that refer to God. When you finish, make a list in your notebook of everything you learn about God and about the spiritual
blessings He bestows on you in Christ. Then take a few min-
utes to thank God for all that He has done for you.

DAY FOUR

Read through Ephesians 1:1-14 again. Reading aloud will
help you better remember what you read. As a matter of fact,
reading something aloud repeatedly will help you memorize it.
If you read a verse or passage aloud three consecutive times,
morning, noon, and night for a week or so, you will soon find it
stored in your memory.

Today as you read, mark every occurrence of the phrase *in
Him (in Christ,*[1] *in Christ Jesus)*. (You will also need to mark
any *in* phrase that refers to Christ, such as *in the Beloved.*[2])
This phrase will tell you what you have "in Christ." You might
want to mark the phrase like this: in Christ and color it
yellow. In this study of Ephesians you do not need to make a
bookmark to list key words. I'll give you instructions on key
words as we move through the book.

Set aside a page or two in your notebook to compile a list of
what you have "in Christ." In the future, whenever you mark a
phrase referring to what you have "in Christ" or "with
Christ," record the insight you gain from marking it on this
page.

---

[1]NIV: *Even Christ* is used in 1:10.
 NKJV: also uses *in Himself, in whom*

[2]NIV: *in the One he loves*

Some of today's work may seem repetitious, but review helps you remember, so know that rewriting some of your insights will only enrich you!

Think about what you have "in Christ," if you are God's child. Tell God how you want to respond to these truths.

DAY FIVE

When you listed what you saw yesterday from marking *in Christ* or *in Him*, you listed that "in Him" you have redemption. The word *redemption* means "to buy or to purchase something." Read Ephesians 1:7,8 and then read 1 Peter 1:18-21. As you read, note who is redeemed, how they are redeemed, what they are redeemed from, and what the result of that redemption is.

Record what you learn in your notebook under the title "Redemption." You may find it helpful to also note which Scripture gave you your insight beside each point in your list. Review your list and take time to thank the Lord Jesus Christ for being willing to redeem you. Talk to Him about how you should live in the light of His sacrifice.

DAY SIX

Read Ephesians 1:1-14 again, looking for the phrase *according to*.[3] Color or mark it in a distinctive way. You may want to simply underline each occurrence of the phrase. When you finish, note what you have or what God has done for you "according to . . .". Also note what it was according to.

Now think about what you have because of God's purpose, His will, His grace. Are you going to believe it?

------

[3]NIV: also *in accordance with*

DAY SEVEN

Store in your heart: Ephesians 1:3,4.

Read and discuss: Ephesians 1:1-8; John 15:16; 1 Peter 1:1,2; Romans 8:28-39. Watch for and, if you choose, mark the words *chose(n)*[4] and *predestined*[5] in these passages.

OPTIONAL QUESTIONS FOR DISCUSSION

∾ From the passages in "Read and discuss" on Day Seven, what do you learn about believers?

∾ From looking at these verses and observing what they say, without adding to them or taking away from what they are saying, Who chose whom? When? Why?

∾ The word *predestined* means "marked out beforehand." According to these passages, do you know why "they" were predestined and what they were predestined for?

∾ Although God chose you for Himself, He still had to redeem you. What did you learn this week about redemption? Discuss any of the 5 W's and an H that are answered for you about redemption in Ephesians and 1 Peter 1:18-21.

∾ How precious are you to God? Remember what you saw in Ephesians 1:1-14 as you answer this question!

∾ Truth sets you free. From all that you read and studied in Ephesians 1, what spoke to your heart the most? Why?

---

[4]KJV; NKJV: *Chosen* is translated *elect* in 1 Peter 1:1,2.

[5]KJV: *predestinated, predestinate*

THOUGHT FOR THE WEEK

So often you are held in bondage to what has been said about you—to man's evaluation or assessment of you, or to your own thoughts or feelings about yourself. When you believe these things and live accordingly, you're held captive by very real but invisible misconceptions. Only truth can set you free and break the chains of the enemy's lies. How you need to know what God says about you—and live accordingly!

God tells you that without faith it is impossible to please Him. God has spoken, and it's all written down in His book, the Bible. God doesn't lie! He can't.

Therefore, my friend, if you are God's child, you are accepted in the Beloved. *You are beloved.* Beloved of God the Father and of Jesus Christ, His Son. You have been blessed with every spiritual blessing in heavenly places. You are part of the church, the body of Jesus Christ. Nothing can or will ever change that.

God is for you, not against you. He chose you for Himself. He marked out beforehand for you to be adopted as His child. Remember this, precious one, no matter how you feel, no matter what anyone says. God is not a liar. He cannot lie. Believe Him. What assurance, what confidence, what security, what peace, what joy, what freedom it will bring.

Secure and Seated
with Jesus!

Day One

Read through Ephesians 1:1-14 a fourth time. Remember, it is helpful to read aloud. Mark any reference you see to the *Holy Spirit.*

When you finish, record in your notebook all you learn from this passage about the Holy Spirit. Be sure to note when you were sealed, what you were sealed with, and what it means to you. Also note how the Holy Spirit is described in verses 13 and 14.

Day Two

Read Ephesians 1:13,14 and Romans 8:9-17. Mark every reference to the *Spirit (Spirit of God, Spirit of Christ, Spirit of Him)* and all pronouns referring to the *Spirit* in the Romans 8 passage. Now add to your list what you learn about the Holy Spirit and His relationship to the believer. If you see a correlation between the verses in Ephesians and Romans, you may want to note the verses as cross-references in the margin of your Bible. Cross-referencing helps when you may not remember the location of a passage that sheds light on or correlates with the one you are studying. Cross-referencing is also very helpful when you do not have your study notes because your notes are right in your Bible! Next to Ephesians 1:13,14 you would write Romans 8:9-17, and next to Romans 8:9-17 you would write Ephesians 1:13,14. That is how you cross-reference!

DAY THREE

Read Ephesians 1:14 and Romans 8:18-23. Mark *redemption* and also mark *Spirit* and its synonyms in the Romans passage.

How do these two passages relate to each other? What do you learn from these verses about the Spirit? What does the Spirit of God have to do with your redemption? Compare this with what you saw in Ephesians 1:7. Note what the Son has to do with your redemption in comparison with the role of the Spirit. Record any new insights on the Holy Spirit or redemption to the lists you are compiling in your notebook.

DAY FOUR

Read Ephesians 1:15-23 aloud. In your notebook list what Paul prays for the Ephesians. Remember, if this is what God laid on Paul's heart to pray for them, it is also on God's heart for you. The Holy Spirit causes us to pray according to the will of God (Romans 8:26,27). (That's another truth about the Holy Spirit!)

DAY FIVE

Read Ephesians 1:15-23 aloud again. In verses 18 and 19 you will notice three occurrences of *what*. I have put the numbers 1, 2, and 3 above these "whats" in my Bible because they list three things that Paul is praying for. Note these and think about them. (If you are using an NIV, you will read in verse 18 the words *in order that you may know.* The three things Paul prays follow this phrase. The NIV does not use the word *what* to precede the three parts of his prayer. You will see these, though, and can mark them 1, 2, 3.) List in your notebook the three things Paul wants them to know.

DAY SIX

Read Ephesians 1:15-23 aloud again. Today focus on verses 18-23. In your notebook draw a simple diagram showing first where Christ is in relationship to God, second where He is in relationship to all rule, authority, power, dominion, and every name, and then where He is in relationship to the church. (In your diagram make sure you show where the church is in relationship to Christ.)

DAY SEVEN

Store in your heart: Ephesians 1:18,19a.
Read and discuss: Acts 19:8-20; Ephesians 1:15-23.

OPTIONAL QUESTIONS FOR DISCUSSION

∾ According to the passage you read in Acts, before the Ephesians came to know the Lord Jesus Christ what were they involved in? Whose power or authority did they seem to be under? What did they do after they believed on the Lord?

∾ Do you see any reason for Paul's prayer in Ephesians 1:15-23? How does what he prayed correspond to what he says to them in these verses? Discuss this.

ᑐ Look at Ephesians 3:10 and Ephesians 6:10-13.

    a. What terms are the same as the passage in Ephesians 1:19-21?

    b. What do you think Paul wants the Ephesians to know and understand? Why?

ᑐ What do you learn from this passage about the believers in Ephesus? How does Paul feel about them?

ᑐ Discuss the elements of Paul's prayer. Discuss specifically what he prays for the "saints at Ephesus" (the church). Discuss what each element of the prayer means and how that knowledge can help believers in their daily walk. When you discuss the second "what" (or point of the prayer), watch whose inheritance it is and where it is.

ᑐ The prayers in the Bible are wonderful prayers for you to use in praying for others. When you pray the Word, you are praying what God would have you pray. In John 15:7, Jesus said that if you abide in Him and His words abide in you, you can ask what you will and it will be done. You might close the discussion by praying this prayer for one another.

THOUGHT FOR THE WEEK

When you come to know the Lord Jesus Christ, you move into another realm spiritually. You become a member of His body, and you are permanently seated with the Lord Jesus Christ in the heavenly places. As you will see next week, this position moves you out from under the dominion of the prince of the power of the air! You are seated above all of Satan's rule, power, authority, and dominion, and above every other name. Now you belong to Jesus! You live under the authority of the name of Jesus Christ, whose name is above all names.

What brought you to this lofty and secure position? It was the power of His resurrection. Jesus Christ was raised from the dead because He conquered sin, Satan, and death. In conquering these, He set you free, redeeming you by His blood. Now, hallelujah, you are bone of His bone, seated with Him in heavenly places. May you live accordingly, fearing no one but Him.

WEEK THREE

Grace That Covers and Provides

DAY ONE

Read through Ephesians 2 and mark the word *formerly*[6] and the phrase *in Christ* (*with Christ, with Him, in Christ Jesus, through Him,*[7] *in whom*[8]). Be sure to mark the phrase the same way you marked it in Ephesians 1. Add your insights to the list you have begun on what you have "in Christ."

DAY TWO

Read Ephesians 2:1-7 aloud. Make a list in your notebook of how you lived "formerly," before you were made alive in Christ. As you make this list, think carefully about what the Bible text says and how those who do not belong to the Lord are described.

DAY THREE

Read Ephesians 2:1,2; John 8:44; John 12:31; and 2 Corinthians 4:3,4. In your notebook list what you learn about

---

[6]NIV: In addition to the word *formerly*, *used to*, *at one time*, and *once* are also used.
 KJV: *in time(s) past, sometimes*
 NKJV: *once*

[7]KJV: *through Christ Jesus*

[8]NIV: *in him*

Satan. You will see him called by several names: the prince of the power of the air,[9] the ruler of this world,[10] the god of this world,[11] the devil, murderer, and liar. This is who ruled your life before the Lord Jesus Christ saved you by His grace. Now do you know why the world is in the state it is in?

DAY FOUR

Read Ephesians 2:1-10 and Titus 3:4-8. Mark the word *grace*. Set aside a page of your notebook for a list on all you will learn in this study of Ephesians about the grace of God. Begin your list by recording everything God has done in His grace according to these passages.

Now read Ephesians 1 again and mark any reference to grace in that chapter. Add your insights to your list!

---

[9]NIV: *the ruler of the kingdom of the air*

[10]NIV; KJV: *the prince of this world*

[11]NIV; NKJV: *the god of this age*

DAY FIVE

Read Ephesians 2:11-18. Take notice of the words *peace* and *enmity*.[12] You may want to underline them. List in your notebook what you learn about the two groups described in this passage. Note what separated them and what made them one.

DAY SIX

Read Ephesians 2 again and mark every occurrence of *you*.[13] Mark the pronouns *we*, *us*, *yourselves*, and *our* in the same way. Then read through the chapter again and make a list in your notebook of everything you learn from marking these words. Review the list and think about all that God has done for you! Surely you will want to thank Him for the lavish grace He has poured on you.

DAY SEVEN

Store in your heart: Ephesians 2:8-10.
Read and discuss: Ephesians 2:1-10; Romans 5:6-11.

OPTIONAL QUESTIONS FOR DISCUSSION

∾ When the New Testament was written, it was written in the Koine Greek. The Greek word for grace is *charis*. It means "unmerited or unearned favor." Read Ephesians 2:8-10.

grace - chairs - the divine influence on the heart

---

[12]NIV: *hostility*

[13]KJV: also uses the word *ye*

    a. How is the definition of grace demonstrated in these verses?

    b. What is contrasted with grace in these verses?

    c. According to this passage, what role do works have in the life of a child of God?

follow faith

∾ Discuss what you learn about the grace of God from Romans 5:6-11. Then read Romans 5:12-21 and see what else these verses tell you about the grace of God.

∾ If you studied Galatians, think about what you learned from that epistle about the grace of God. What was the Galatians' problem?

∾ Read Paul's words in 1 Corinthians 15:9,10 and note Paul's reference to the grace of God. According to these verses, how was grace demonstrated in Paul's life? How did Paul respond to the grace of God? How does this parallel with Ephesians 2:8-10?

NO

∾ Is grace a license to sin, to live any way you want to live? Read Jude 3,4 and note what some people will do with the grace of God and how these people are described. How are you to respond to the grace of God?

faith

∾ What are you depending on to get you to heaven? According to what you have read in Ephesians, will it work?

THOUGHT FOR THE WEEK

Are you bowed to the ground, unable to look up because of the weight of guilt or sin you're carrying? Christ Jesus came into the world to save sinners. You are not alone. All have sinned and fallen short of the glory ("the true estimate") of God (Romans 3:23). Yes, you who were created in God's image have desecrated that image and failed to give a true estimate of the character of God in your life. But, Beloved, Christ came to save you! Like all mankind, you are born dead in trespasses and sins. Because of sin, you have walked your own way. Like all of us, you have followed your lusts and walked under the power of the devil. But Jesus Christ brings all that to an end when you turn to Him, when you acknowledge that He is God and that He has a right to rule your life.

The minute you simply believe, the minute you receive Jesus Christ as your Savior and Lord and acknowledge Him as God, you are saved by the grace of God. You are saved, but not saved to live as you please. Rather you are saved so that you can walk in the good works that God has ordained for you. Works that He has planned especially for you. For example, one of the works God has ordained for me is to teach people how to study the Word of God. This book is part of His calling on my life. The good works vary, but they all have their source in God.

Don't miss these good works by focusing on your past, your sin, your failures, or by excusing yourself from serving God because of what you were or what was done to you. If I did that, I would never be doing what I am doing now because my past is not a pretty one. You must choose, as I did, to believe God, to say with Paul, "By the grace of God I am what I am" (1 Corinthians 15:10). His grace toward me will not be in vain. Rather, I am going to walk out of the prison of my past and live in freedom. Yet it is not going to be me, but the grace of God in me! I am going to appropriate that all-sufficient, more-than-abundant, lavish grace.

O my friend, free yourself from that load of guilt. Where sin abounded, grace did much more abound. You are without excuse. Appropriate His grace and press on!

Loved Unconditionally

DAY ONE

Read through Ephesians 3. Remember to read aloud because that will help you remember the content of Ephesians. Mark the word *mystery*. The Greek word for *mystery* is *musterion*. A mystery is a spiritual truth that was previously hidden and not revealed until God chose to explain it through one of His servants.

DAY TWO

Read Ephesians 2:19–3:7. Note who the "you"[14] is in 2:19. Are they Gentiles or Jews? Ephesians 2 makes the answer clear. Maybe you noted this insight as you studied last week.

When you finish reading today's passage, see if you can discern what the mystery is that Paul revealed. Write what you decide in your notebook. Be very clear when you write it out.

If you have time, read Ephesians 1:1-14 again and note the context in which the word *mystery* is used. What do you learn? (Marking *mystery* throughout your Bible in the same distinctive way you mark it in Ephesians will enable you to learn lots of mysteries!)

---

[14]KJV: *ye*

DAY THREE

Read Ephesians 3 again aloud. This time mark the word *grace* in the same way that you marked it in Ephesians 1 and 2. Add what you learn about grace from this chapter to your list. As you do, carefully observe the grace God gave Paul and what God's grace enabled him to do.

DAY FOUR

Read Ephesians 3 again. Mark the phrase *in Christ Jesus, in whom,* or any reference to being "in Christ"[15] as you have done before. Then add what you learn to your "in Christ" list in your notebook.

DAY FIVE

As you survey Ephesians, it is so important to keep the entire message before you. In the first three chapters of Ephesians, Paul deals with the believer's position in Christ. Paul uses certain key words to help him convey his point. Read Ephesians 1 and 3 again and watch for the word *purpose(d)*. In a survey course like this, you may not understand the depth of all Paul is saying, but what do you learn about God's purpose as it relates to you, His child?

What does this tell you about you, Beloved? Is your life meaningless to God? Live according to what God's Word says.

DAY SIX

Read Ephesians 3:14-21. Mark the words *Spirit, power,*[16] and *love.* When you mark the word *power,* go back and mark

---

[15]KJV: also uses *in Christ, by Christ*

[16]KJV; NKJV: also uses *might*

power in Ephesians 1:19 in the same way. I mark the word *love* with a heart like this ♥ , and then I color it red. You may also want to mark *love(d)* in the same way in Ephesians 1:4 and 2:4. Do you know how loved you are, and by whom?

When you finish, list in your notebook the specific things Paul prays for the church at Ephesus.

How would you summarize the content of each of the first three chapters of Ephesians? What is the main theme or subject of each? Record the theme of each chapter on the EPHESIANS AT A GLANCE chart (page 87) under the proper chapter number. Also fill in any other information as you can. Filling in this chart will give you a ready reference to an overview of the book when it is complete.

DAY SEVEN

Store in your heart: Ephesians 3:20,21.
Read and discuss: Ephesians 1:22,23; 2:19-22; 3:8-10,20,21.

OPTIONAL QUESTIONS FOR DISCUSSION

∾ What is the mystery Paul reveals in Ephesians 2 but specifically calls a mystery in chapter 3?

   a. How did this mystery come about? In other words, what did God or Jesus do to bring it about?

   b. Where does it place the Jew and the Gentile?

   c. What kind of a temple are we?

   d. Where are we seated and why?

   e. What role does the Spirit play in this mystery? (See Ephesians 2:18-22.)

∾ Discuss what Paul prays for the church in Ephesians 3.

   a. How have you seen the love of God manifested in Ephesians 1–3? Or to put it another way, what shows you the depth and breadth of God's love in these chapters?

   b. According to this prayer in Ephesians 3, where does Christ dwell and how?

   c. This is Paul's second prayer for the Ephesians. Remember, the first prayer is recorded in Ephesians 1:15-23. You will notice that power is mentioned in both prayers. What does Paul want the believers at Ephesus to know? What does God want you to know?

   d. To whom is this power available? How are you strengthened by this power? Where? Consider both prayers as you answer these questions.

   e. How can Christ do exceeding abundantly above all you ask or think?

   f. What have you learned about the Spirit from marking the references to Him in Ephesians 1–3?

∾ Look at what you have listed on the page in your notebook titled "In Christ." How has knowing these things about your position in Christ personally ministered to you?

∾ What have you learned from Ephesians 1–3 about the grace of God?

∾ What has spoken to you the most in these first three chapters of Ephesians?

THOUGHT FOR THE WEEK

Paul prayed that the Ephesians would recognize and know with a certainty what was theirs because they were Christ's. They were a part of His body, His temple, in which He dwelt by His Spirit. And this, Beloved, is my prayer for you, because it is what God wants you to know. This is why He had Paul write what he did. To know and understand this is to be secure in the love of God and of Christ. Nothing is more freeing than to know that you are loved, unconditionally and forever. Such knowledge of this love fills you up with the fullness of God.

But not only does God want you to comprehend the breadth and length and height and depth of His love, He also wants you to know the surpassing power that works in you. It is resurrection power that God brought about in Jesus when He raised Jesus from the dead. It is the power of the Holy Spirit that is there to strengthen you in your inner man. It is His power that is at work in you. His power enables you to live a supernatural life as a man or woman of God. It is a life beyond your own wisdom or abilities. It is a life that brings God glory and that gives a true picture (a true estimate) of the character of God.

How the world, how your associates, need to see His life lived out in you! This is possible, Beloved, because you are in Christ and He is in you. Never forget that!

Forgiven—
and Able to Forgive!

DAY ONE

Read Ephesians 4. Mark every reference to the *Spirit* as you have done previously. (Make sure it is a reference to the Holy Spirit.) Also mark the word *redemption* and every occurrence of the word *walk*.[17] Note the change in the epistle at this point. What does Paul begin to do at this point in his letter to the Ephesians? Keep adding insights to your list on redemption.

DAY TWO

Read Ephesians 4:1-6 aloud. Mark the word *one*. Then list in your notebook all that Christians have in the unity of the Spirit and how they are to walk.

DAY THREE

Read Ephesians 4:1-16 aloud. Mark *grace* as you have done previously. Also mark every use of the word *gift(s)* in a distinctive way. Then on a page in your notebook write the heading

---

[17]NIV: *live*

"Spiritual Gifts" and list what you learn from this passage in Ephesians about the gifts that are mentioned. Note who gave them, to whom, when they were given, and why they were given. Remember, too, to add insights to your list on the grace of God.

DAY FOUR

Read Ephesians 4:11-16 aloud. Mark every occurrence of the word *body* and every reference to *the saints*,[18] including any pronouns or synonyms. Then list in your notebook what you learn about the saints and the body from this passage. As you compile your list, ask the 5 W's and an H. For example, "How is the body built up?" "What are the saints to attain to?" "What will happen if they attain this?"

DAY FIVE

Read Ephesians 4:17-24. Mark the phrase *old self*.[19] Then contrast the way the Gentiles walk with what those who are in Christ are to do. You may want to record this contrasting list in your notebook. You might also want to record this list in the margin of your Bible or note it in some way so you can easily spot it.

DAY SIX

Read Ephesians 4:17-32. Did you see the "therefore"[20] in verse 25? Whenever you see a "therefore," find out what it is there for. I mark *therefore* with three red dots like this: ∴ . Now you will want to see what this therefore is there for. First

---

[18]NIV: *God's people*

[19]KJV; NKJV: *old man*

[20]KJV; NKJV: *wherefore*

mark the word in your Bible. Then consider Ephesians 4:25-32 and make a list in your notebook of how you are to behave now that you have put on the new self.

Record the main theme of Ephesians 4 on the EPHE-SIANS AT A GLANCE chart (page 87).

DAY SEVEN

♥ Store in your heart: Ephesians 4:1-3; Ephesians 4:32; or Ephesians 4:1,32.

Read and discuss: Ephesians 4:22-32 and Colossians 3:12-14.

OPTIONAL QUESTIONS FOR DISCUSSION

[handwritten margin note: deal with anger immediately]

∾ When you developed your list from Ephesians 4:25-32 of how we are to behave, what did you write down? Look at each thing separately and discuss one by one the things you are to do. Then examine yourself and ask yourself these questions: Am I doing what God says to do? If not, why not?

∾ Is there anyone you haven't forgiven? Why is that?

∾ How much has the Lord Jesus Christ forgiven you? *Totally*

∾ What is the difference between offending another person and offending the Lord Jesus Christ? Who is perfect, with- *JC* out sin? Would your offense toward man or toward God seem greater? Why? *sin is sin if it contravenes God's Law / love one another*

∾ According to Ephesians 4:32, how are you to forgive others? Are there any conditions to this forgiveness? Are there transgressions or sins that you don't have to forgive others for because of how bad, cruel, or unloving they have been to you? *as JC forgave — no conditions*

∾ Read Colossians 3:12-14 again. How do these verses parallel what God says in Ephesians? *almost word for word*

〰 If you refuse to forgive others, what happens to you? Look
up the following verses and discuss them: Matthew 6:12-15
and Matthew 18:21-35.

〰 According to what you have learned about your position
in Christ, do you have the power, the ability, to forgive?
Where is that power? How is it yours? If you have it and
don't use it, then are you walking as God called you to
walk? If you don't walk as God called you to walk, what are
you doing?

〰 Are you, Beloved, willing to obey the Lord in the matters
set forth in Ephesians 4? If not, why not?

THOUGHT FOR THE WEEK

The entire body of Jesus Christ is made up of people who
have been forgiven all their sins. And if you are part of His
body, you have been forgiven not because you deserve it or
because you have earned the right to be forgiven, but simply
because of the unconditional, lavish, undeserved, unearned
grace of God that He bestowed on you freely in Christ Jesus,
His beloved Son.

You deserve condemnation, but there is no condemnation
to those who are in Christ Jesus. That's where you are if you
belong to Him.

If you, who have sinned against a holy, blameless God,
have been forgiven so very much, how can you withhold forgiveness from others because of the debt you feel they owe you
and because of their sin against you? To withhold forgiveness is
to act contrary to all that you understand about the gospel of
your salvation, which is the forgiveness of your sins, your
debts, from a holy God. To refuse to forgive is to deny or forget
what salvation is all about. It is to play God and to say, "God
would forgive you, but I won't. Your sin is too great!"

Beloved, listen carefully. If you refuse to forgive, you are like the person in the story Jesus told in Matthew 18. Until you forgive, you are going to be held in a prison of your own making. You are going to be given over to the "torturers," so to speak. In other words, you are going to feel tormented until you walk in obedience and forgive others. If you are a child of God, you can forgive because you have His Spirit and His power. Do not grieve the Holy Spirit of God.

How Can I
Walk in Love?

Day One

Read Ephesians 5 and mark every occurrence of the words *walk*[21] and *love* (*loved, loves*).

Day Two

Read Ephesians 5:1-6; 1 Corinthians 6:9-11; and Galatians 5:19-21. In each of these passages you might want to underline or mark in some way any reference to *inheriting the kingdom of God*. Then in your notebook list what you learn from these passages about those who won't inherit the kingdom of God.

Day Three

Read Ephesians 5:7-14. Note the contrast between light and darkness. List in your notebook what the children of the light are to do.

Day Four

Read Ephesians 5:1-21 to keep the context fresh in your mind, but concentrate on verses 15-21. Contrast the wise with

---

[21]NIV: *live*

the unwise. How are the wise to walk? List in your notebook exactly what this passage says the wise are to do. Then examine your walk with the Lord in the light of this. Are you walking as a wise person?

DAY FIVE

Read Ephesians 5:15-33 and concentrate on 5:22-33. Note in Ephesians 5:22-33 how husbands and wives are to live. Where does the power to do so come from? What is the command of Ephesians 5:18?

In your notebook, list exactly what wives are told to do. As you list these things, don't forget to examine them in the light of the 5 W's and an H. If you are a married woman, examine your walk in the light of these verses.

Does God tell you to submit only if your husband loves you as Christ loves the church? Who will give you the power to submit?

DAY SIX

Read Ephesians 5:22-33 again. This time focus on God's word to the husbands. In your notebook list exactly what husbands are to do. Note the why and the how of the instructions. Also mark every reference to *Christ (Lord, He Himself, Savior, He, Himself, His)*. Then make a list of what you learn about the Lord from these verses. If you are a husband, examine your walk in the light of these verses. Are these words conditional? Does this passage say you are to love your wife in this way if she is submissive and respects you? Does this passage command you to make your wife submit to you?

Record the main theme of Ephesians 5 on the EPHESIANS AT A GLANCE chart (page 87).

DAY SEVEN

Store in your heart: Ephesians 5:2.

Read and discuss: Ephesians 5:1-14 and 1 Corinthians 13:1-3.

OPTIONAL QUESTIONS FOR DISCUSSION

∾ It seems easier to *say* "I love you" to God, to your mate, or to your fellowman than it is to *walk* in love. What did you learn from Ephesians 5 about walking in love?

a. Drawing from what you have studied in Ephesians, if you walk in love, how will you walk with respect to
1) God?
2) your mate?
3) your fellowman?

b. According to 1 Corinthians 13, if you don't walk in love, what is the end result? In 1 Corinthians 13:1-3, you see a list of things you may have or do, but what do they profit if you do not love?

∾ According to Ephesians 5, what is the believer's pattern or example for walking in love? *:1 imitate god.*

a. To what degree does that love go?

b. To what degree is a husband's love for his wife to go? Under what conditions?

∾ What or who will give you the love you need in order to love others? Read Galatians 5:22. How would all this compare with the command in Ephesians 5:18?

∾ According to Ephesians 5:22, the wife is to be subject to her own husband. However, according to Ephesians 5, is the wife the only one who is to be in submission?

∾ In your study this week, what did you learn about those who will not inherit the kingdom of God? In the passages you studied in Day Two, did you notice the repeated warning not to be deceived? What does this tell you about those who are really children of God?

∾ What verse or verses spoke to you the most in Ephesians 5? What are you going to do with what God has said?

THOUGHT FOR THE WEEK

How can a wife submit to a husband who doesn't love her with a sacrificial love? How can a husband love, nurture, and cherish a wife who has so many shortcomings?

The answer to these and other hard questions is found in one verse, Ephesians 5:18: "Keep on being filled with the Holy Spirit."

The Holy Spirit is there, living within. You are sealed in Him until the day of your redemption. Christ is in you, and you are in Him. You have the Spirit. You have His resurrection power! Now walk in the light of it. Walk in love. Be filled with the Spirit. He is there, and He is longing to fill you, waiting to fill you.

The fruit of His filling will be ninefold: love, joy, peace, patience, kindness, goodness, faithfulness, gentleness, and self-control (Galatians 5:22,23).

Because the command to "be filled with the Spirit" is in the passive voice, it means that the Spirit will do the filling if you will only allow Him.

So know this, dear child of God, you can be what God commands you to be. You can do what God commands you to do. All because you have the Spirit of God. So let Him do what He has been called to do. No word of God is void of power. He will give you His power to be the wife, the husband—and, as you will see in Ephesians 6—the child, the parent, the employer, the employee, or the soldier He has called you to be. It's all a matter of faith's obedience. Be filled with His Spirit, Beloved.

Stand Firm!

Day One

Read Ephesians 6 to get a good overview of this final and important chapter. Mark the words *Spirit* and *mystery*.

Day Two

Read Ephesians 6:1-4; Exodus 20:12; and Deuteronomy 5:16; 6:1-9. List in your notebook what you learn from these passages about how a child is to behave toward his parents and the responsibilities of the father to his child.

Day Three

Read Ephesians 6:5-9; 1 Peter 2:18-25; and James 5:1-6. Then record in your notebook what you learn from these passages about the servant and the master (the rich man in James) by listing their responsibilities and how they are to respond to each other. Think about this list in the light of the relationship between employer and employee. How do you measure up?

Read Ephesians 6:1-9 again and think of how different our society would be if we really heeded these words from God. It is our responsibility to live as God tells us to live, no matter what others do or say.

DAY FOUR

Read Ephesians 6:10-17 aloud. Then read the passage again and mark every reference to the *devil*. Mark *the rulers*,[22] *the powers*,[23] *the world forces of darkness*,[24] and *the spiritual forces of wickedness in heavenly places*[25] in the same way, because all of these are under the domain of the prince of the power of the air, the devil. Revelation 12:7-9 makes it clear that there is a whole host of angelic beings that follow Satan and do his bidding. These are the unseen rulers, the powers, the world and spiritual forces who oppose the work of God on earth. Then, list in your notebook what you learn from marking these words.

DAY FIVE

Read Ephesians 6:10-17 aloud again. This is one passage you should memorize. Mark every occurrence of *stand firm*.[26] Then in your notebook list every instruction given to the

---

[22]KJV; NKJV: *principalities*

[23]NIV: *the authorities*

[24]NIV: *the powers of this dark world*
  KJV: *the rulers of the darkness of this world*
  NKJV: *the rulers of the darkness of this age*

[25]NIV: *the spiritual forces of evil in the heavenly realms*
  KJV: *spiritual wickedness in high places*
  NKJV: *spiritual hosts of wickedness in the heavenly places*

[26]NIV: also uses *take your stand, stand your guard*
  KJV: *stand, withstand*
  NKJV: also uses *stand against*

recipients of this letter you find as a result of marking this phrase. As you look at these instructions, study the picture on page 84. This visual aid, which allows you to see each part of a Roman soldier's armor, will help you greatly in understanding the meaning behind what Paul says.[27]

DAY SIX

Read Ephesians 6:18-24. Mark the words *prayer*,[28] *pray*, and *petition*[29] in the same way. Also mark the word *love*. Then in your notebook list what you learn about prayer from this passage. When you finish, stop and think about the importance of prayer. Would Paul have prayed what he prayed for the Ephesians, or would he have asked for prayer, if prayer didn't make a difference?

Record the main theme of Ephesians 6 on the EPHESIANS AT A GLANCE chart (page 87). Then record the main theme of the book of Ephesians on the chart in the appropriate place.

DAY SEVEN

♥ Store in your heart: Ephesians 6:13, or preferably Ephesians 6:10-12.

Read and discuss: Ephesians 6:10-20; 1 Peter 5:8,9; 2 Corinthians 11:2-4,13-15.

---

[27]For more help in understanding spiritual warfare, see Kay's book *Lord, Is It Warfare? Teach Me to Stand* (Multnomah).

[28]NIV; KJV; NKJV: also use *praying*

[29]NIV: *requests*
KJV; NKJV: *supplication*

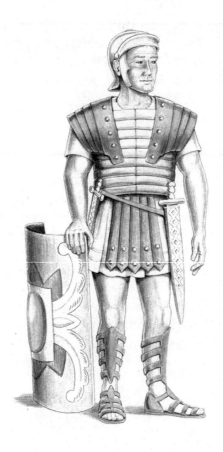

OPTIONAL QUESTIONS FOR DISCUSSION

∾ No other epistle has as much to say about warfare as the book of Ephesians. Review once again the background of the church at Ephesus. In the light of this background, wouldn't it seem logical that Paul would stress the Ephesians' need to remember who they are and where they are seated—and that they need to stand firm in the Lord and in the strength of His might?

(margin notes: committed, R+, bound R+, interal, flesh, prepared)

✑ What do you learn from Paul's prayer in Ephesians 1 that parallels with his words in Ephesians 6:10-17? Watch the use of the words "strength of His might"[30] and "power."

✑ What do you see in both passages about "the strength of His might"?

✑ What conflict of power do you see in Ephesians 1 and Ephesians 6? Which conflict is greater? How do you know this from the text?

✑ What are God's general instructions to the believer in Ephesians 6:10-17 concerning warfare?

✑ What are the specific pieces of the armor that are to be "put on"? Name them. As you do, discuss what each piece of armor represents in the Christian life. For example, it is the belt of __Truth__, the breastplate of _Righteousness_, etc. What is God showing you that is going to combat the schemes of the devil? _Helmet of Salvation_

✑ What are the specific pieces of armor that the child of God is to "take up"[31]? Name these pieces of armor and then describe what each piece represents, as you just did in the previous question. _Shield of Faith / Word of God, the Sword_

✑ How many offensive weapons does the child of God have?

   a. What are they or is it?   _WOG_

   b. What does this show you about combating the enemy? What are you to use? _Scripture_

   c. How does this compare with John 8:44? _WOG = Truth / Lie of Satan_

   d. How would all this go with the passage you read in 2 Corinthians 11:2-4,13-15?

   Stand firm on Scripture - Truth of God

---

[30]NIV: *his mighty strength, his mighty power*
   KJV; NKJV: *his mighty power, the power of his might*   _Christ is Truth_

[31]NIV: also uses *put on*
   KJV: also uses *take unto you, taking*   _Satan is Lie_

Christ

_(me)_

focus understanding

e. How important then is making regular Bible study a habit, as you are doing in this *International Inductive Study Series*? What is this study helping you do?

∾ How does 1 Peter 5:8,9 go with what you learned in Ephesians about warfare? *Paul/Peter say something be prepared/watch*

∾ How does one build his faith? *walk & trust God*

∾ What place do you think prayer has in spiritual warfare? Could it be your "walkie-talkie," so that as you go to battle you remember to stay in communication with General Command Headquarters? How essential is it?

∾ Well, our study of Ephesians has come to a close.

a. What has ministered to you the most in these seven weeks of study?

b. What truths from Ephesians have liberated you and freed you from bondage? *How* have these truths freed you from bondage?

THOUGHT FOR THE WEEK

Life is filled with conflicts. One major conflict is the battle for your mind, your beliefs, your thoughts, the standards by which you choose to live, and the principles for which you are willing to die.

You once lived under the dominion of the prince of the power of the air. You walked under his domain according to the lusts of the flesh and the desires of your mind. But then you met Truth, the Lord Jesus Christ, and He set you free and seated you in heavenly places and blessed you with every spiritual blessing that you will ever need to live as more than a conqueror.

The enemy would seek to have you forget that your warfare is not with flesh and blood. He would love to get you to fight against him in the strength of your own flesh. He would love to have you warring against him without your armor. He would love to have you out of touch, out of communication with the Captain of the Hosts.

Be alert, be vigilant. The battle is not going to lessen. These are the last days. The enemy's time is short and he knows it. He's desperate, but he's defeated. Don't ever forget that. So put on the armor of God daily. Keep girding your loins with God's Word. His Word is pure, unadulterated truth. Protect your vital organs with the breastplate of righteousness. Stay away from sin. Live the way God says to live. Be filled with the Spirit.

God tells you to walk by the Spirit so you will not fulfill the lusts of your flesh. Walk in those sandals of peace. Remember, you are at peace with God. Jesus won that peace at Calvary. Stand in that assurance. Take the shield of faith. The more you know of the whole counsel of God, the greater will be your shield. It will be easier and easier to put out the fiery arrows the evil one hurls at you. Take that helmet of salvation. Remember to whom you belong. Don't ever forget it! And because you belong to Christ and He is in you, then greater is He who is in you than he who is in the world.

Finally, get your sword out of its sheath. Lift it high. It's the sword of the Lord—the Word of God. It's the same sword that will come out of Jesus' mouth when He comes to reign on this earth as King of kings and Lord of lords.

The Captain of the Hosts is coming! Occupy until He comes. Soon you'll even be free from Satan's attacks, for he will be thrown into the lake of fire to be punished forever. But you will spend eternity in the city of our God!

Theme of Ephesians:

Author: Paul

Date:

Purpose:

Key Words:

SEGMENT DIVISIONS			CHAPTER THEMES
		1	
		2	
		3	
		4	
		5	
		6	

THE INTERNATIONAL INDUCTIVE STUDY BIBLE IS

Changing the Way People Study God's Word

*I*T IS A REVOLUTIONARY IDEA whose time has come....a study Bible that actually teaches you *how* to study the Bible. As you follow simple, easy-to-understand instructions, you will discover God's truth on your own. In *The International Inductive Study Bible*, you will find maps right in the text where you need them, timeline charts showing biblical events in historical order, wide margins in which to write your notes, the accurate and reliable New American Standard Bible text, and dozens of other helpful features. This proven study method will lead you to experience God's Word in a way so personal, so memorable, that every insight you gain will be yours for life.

HARVEST HOUSE PUBLISHERS
1075 Arrowsmith, Eugene OR 97402
At bookstores everywhere!

Books in the
International Inductive Study Series

Teach Me Your Ways
Genesis, Exodus, Leviticus, Numbers, Deuteronomy

Choosing Victory, Overcoming Defeat
Joshua, Judges, Ruth

God's Blueprint for Bible Prophecy
Daniel

The Call to Follow Jesus
Luke

The Holy Spirit Unleashed in You
Acts

God's Answers for Relationships and Passions
1 & 2 Corinthians

Free from Bondage God's Way
Galatians, Ephesians

Standing Firm in These Last Days
1 & 2 Thessalonians

Behold, Jesus Is Coming!
Revelation

Also by Kay Arthur

How to Study Your Bible

❧

Beloved

❧

His Imprint, My Expression

❧

My Savior, My Friend

❧

God, Are You There?

❧

Lord, Teach Me to Pray in 28 Days

❧

With an Everlasting Love

❧

Israel, My Beloved

❏ **YES!** I am interested in information that will direct me to an Inductive Bible study group in my area *or that* will help me or my church become involved in inductive Bible study.

❏ I am interested in further training on how to study my Bible inductively. Please send me information on how to know God and His Word in a more personal way.

I have used this book

❏ in personal devotions and/or study

❏ in Sunday school

❏ in small group study

❏ in church

❏ in the community

❏ in connection with the radio program, "Precept with Kay Arthur."

❏ I have received Jesus Christ as my Lord and Savior as a result of this study. Please send me literature that will help me become established in God's Word.

Name of this book _____

Name _____

Address _____

City/State/Zip _____

Daytime telephone (_____) _____

 Precept Ministries exists for the sole purpose of establishing God's people in His Word. We desire to help you minister more effectively to others.